Spindrift Memories

Joan Callahan Hulse
Ed Sullivan

BOOKSIDE Press

Spindrift Memories © 2022
Joan Callahan Hulse
Ed Sullivan

All rights reserved. No part of this publication may be reproduced, distributed, or transmitted in any form or by any means, including photocopying, recording, or other electronic or mechanical methods, without the prior written permission of the publisher, except in the case brief quotations embodied in critical reviews and other noncommercial uses permitted by copyright law.

ISBN:
Paperback   978-1-998784-53-0

The views expressed in this book are solely those of the author and do not necessarily reflect the views of the publisher, and the publisher hereby disclaims any responsibility for them.

BookSide Press
877-741-8091
www.booksidepress.com
orders@booksidepress.com

Contents

Day Two **9**

Day Three *27*

Day Four *45*

Day Five *61*

Day Six *81*

Hi there! My name is Ryan and I love sharing happy memories. I love to enjoy special times all over again in my mind. And I hope you enjoy this too.

My sister, Emma and I spent many happy visits at the seashore with our Uncle Ed, who helped us appreciate this world of wonder. "Spindrift Memories" is about the first time our parents had finally agreed that we were old enough to spend the week alone with Uncle Ed. I still smile when I remember the fun we had. We continue to visit as often as possible. The seashore is a captivating place that is exciting and peaceful at the same time.

Although years have passed since the invitation affived, I remember the day clearly. Bored after three weeks of summer vacation, Emma and I were sitting on the front porch playing a game of cards. Mr. Taylor, the mailman, approached with a cheery, "got a letter for you two. It looks important."

SPINDRIFT MEMORIES

We immediately recognized the bold writing on the envelope. Uncle Ed often sent us notes or greeting cards and they were always fun to receive. But today's note held a special excitement. It read:

> Dear Emma and Ryan,
> Please come visit me at the shore.
> You 'll get to love it more and more.
> Each day differs from the last,
> The beach, the water and all things past.
>
> We 'll swim, we 'll fish, we 'll lie in the sun
> And be dog-tired when day is done.
> We 'll see strange little animals all in shells
> And hear the sea crunch, and smell clean smells.
>
> We 'll write and talk and draw
> All the wonderful things
> We felt and found and saw.
>
> So please come down and see my world
> Of water and air and sand and life.
> The world itself seems to start each day here.
> You 'll see it happen in a big orange sphere.
>   (Guess what that is?)
>   Uncle Ed
>
> P.S. Have Mom or Dad call me for the details.
> Hope to see you Saturday.

Waving the letter, we ran to tell Mom.

Emma and I were very excited at the thought of a visit to the shore. We packed our bags and they sat waiting for three long days while time seemed to stand still. But Saturday finally arrived and on a beautiful summer day Mom and Dad drove us to the shore.

As we neared our destination, we tried to remember the area. We had been younger when we last visited Uncle Ed at his beach house, but familiar things began to appear. Ahead was the water tower, off a little distance was the church steeple with its bell, then the post office and grocery store. In a minute we would turn into the sandy lane scattered with weather-worn cottages that looked so inviting.

Lucky Lane! There it was. And at the end of the lane would be Uncle Ed's house nestled behind the dunes.

Uncle Ed's house was a simple one that had braved many storms. Seeing it again gave us a warm, secure feeling Dad pulled up beside the little driftwood sign that read—Spindrift.

We had arrived! And there was Uncle Ed to welcome us. Warm handshakes and hugs were passed around as we scrambled out of the car. Uncle Ed put an arm around each of us and remarked, "I'm sure everyone tells you — my, how you've grown! And it's true. It won't be long before you are both all grown- up. I've really been looking forward to your visit. We're going to have a good time together."

Uncle Ed had packed a picnic lunch to eat by the water's edge and soon we were all down on the beach enjoying the waves as they broke over us, feeling the sun on our backs and the sand soft under our feet. It was just the right place for Dad to voice his favorite expression, "this is the life!"

While Mom and Dad shared the latest family news with Uncle Ed, Emma and I had fun building an elaborate sand castle complete with turrets and moats. The afternoon passed quickly and too soon we collected our beach stuff and headed back to Spindrift.

We said good-bye to our parents shortly after dinner and returned to the beach. We walked in silence for a few minutes looking, listening. "The beach," said Uncle Ed, "has many moods and hopefully you will enjoy some of them on your visit.

Many things are part of a mood. The weather, the tides, the time of day, the season of the year and your individual feelings all combine and blend to create an ever-changing, never- quite the- same picture."

Already we could see that the mood of the beach had changed. It was no longer the crowded, hot place of the afternoon. Our ears, too, had become tuned to the different sounds we were hearing — the lap of the waves when the tide is low, the thunder of waves at high tide, the harsh cry of the gull, Now the beach was very quiet, with just a murmur of a breeze. Listening carefully, we could even hear the dune grasses rubbing and brushing together. Sounds of sea and sounds of land melted together.

Walking slowly along the edge of the water, it seemed very different from this afternoon. The sun getting low in the sky spread a happy pink glow over the sand. Sea gulls were busy doing their job of cleaning the beach. They didn't seem to mind our presence at all. The tide was now low; it had left our sand castle to guard the shore.

As we walked, we gathered shells until our pockets were heavy with their weight. With a laugh, Uncle Ed said, "You remind me of my daughters when they were young. They would fill their pockets and pails, their hats and hands. But you will soon learn to collect only the more perfect shells. In the beginning the great numbers of shells are hard to pass by; you will want to have them all."

Our feet automatically led us back to Spindrift where we marveled at the many sea treasures throughout the house that we had been too busy to appreciate in the afternoon. Uncle Ed had collected them over many years and from many different beaches.

Lovely shells lined the window sills, each one beautiful in its own special way. There were jars of beach glass, worn smooth by the sand and waves. Other jars held beach glass in tiny jagged pieces resembling a jewel — all that remained after being battered against a rocky shoreline. Driftwood, with its twisted shapes, decorated many corners. There were things with strange names, like whelk egg cases, sand dollars, sea urchins, star fish and so many more treasures from the sea.

We would spend much time during the next few days examining each piece, wondering about its age, place of birth, how much of the ocean it had seen. We wished these little gems could talk, they had so much to share.

Uncle Ed could see our fascination with his treasures. "Let's have a little game," he said. "Here are pencils and paper. Now suppose that you were designing the inhabitants of the sea and the shore. What would they look like?"

For a few minutes, we sat quiet and thoughtless. "I'm not sure I know what you mean," said Emma hesitantly. "Can you give us a clue?"

"Be glad to," said Uncle Ed. "In fact, I'll give you a few clues. Think of the beach and the shore and the kind of surroundings that your sea creatures must face. The waves will pound away at their homes. Tides will leave the sand of the beach under water part of the time and then expose it to the burning sun and scavenging birds part of the time. Many of the sea creatures wear their skeletons on the outside to protect their soft bodies Don't forget to give your creatures a way of eating, remembering that some move about while others live most of their life in one place."

"Oh! Now I know what you mean," I said and began sketching. In a short time, we had dozens of strange looking things that combined those features we already knew with other features straight from our imagination.

"Great work!" said Uncle Ed as he examined our efforts. "Emma, I see that you've made the bodies and shells quite streamlined and smooth. That will allow water to roll off easily and waves won't disturb them too much .0n this one you have good suction cup feet. You won't have to worry about him getting washed off his favorite rock.

Yours are different, but equally good, Ryan. Those claws are going to ensure that this fellow doesn't go hungry. I like the waving tentacles on this one, too. He'll be able to capture the tiny food in the sea water as it passes by.

I just noticed something. All of your creatures seem to be looking for a meal. I think you're trying to tell me something. How about a snack before bedtime?"

"I am sort of hungry," I said with a grateful grin.

We enjoyed cookies and milk while we looked through some of Uncle Ed's many books about the sea. "Some of these things are like our drawings," said Emma in surprise.

"Yes, they are," said Uncle Ed. "It's hard to design something that nature hasn't already thought of— no matter how strange you make it. Some of these fellows live in the deep sea and we won't find them on the beach. But it will be fun to check your ideas against the sea animals that we do find.

Look at the time! Your Mother probably thinks that you have been asleep for an hour. Off to bed with you now."

It had been an exciting day. We were tired but it was that nice "happy tired" feeling. Sleep came easily for us. The rhythm of the waves was a lullaby to two sleepy children.

Day Two

Sunlight danced warmly across our bedroom. It seemed to be inviting us out to enjoy this lovely, absolutely brand- new day.

At home Mom always had a problem getting us up in the morning, but today we jumped out of bed ready and eager for the fun of discovery that the day promised.

"Good morning, sleepyheads," said Uncle Ed enthusiastically as he sat sipping coffee on the front porch. "How about a walk on the beach before breakfast?"

"Let's go," I said, starting for the beach with Emma right behind.

"Wait for me," laughed Uncle Ed putting down his coffee cup. "Remember it was my idea."

It was a beautiful day The sun sparkled on the water. A flock of noisy gulls circled in a cloudless sky. The tide was almost low, as it had been the evening before.

All around was the smell of the beach at low tide. It was a unique smell, one that we would learn to love. This smell was a mixture of wet sand, sea animals and plants, and salt evaporated from the water. To those familiar with this unique aroma, it means just one thing — the beach.

Uncle Ed looked thoughtful. "I like to start my day here. Sometimes I walk, sometimes I just sit and absorb the sights, the sounds, the smells. For me the beach and the ocean are things of fascination and beauty. I never tire of them.

I try to remember that every drop of water is brimming with life; that nothing in the sea lives only for itself, but is linked with all, living and dead. Each creature is necessary to the life of the sea, from the tiny diatoms to the huge whales. Each makes the sea live and supports life. A quart of sea water may contain 3,000 different kinds of larvae at one time, each one important though microscopically small.

We still have so much to learn about the sea and its life. If I had one wish it would be that people everywhere learn to respect this place of beauty and mystery."

We walked in silence for a few minutes, each thinking his own thoughts about Uncle Ed's wish. I knew that people would learn to love the sea and the shore if they could live there for a time with Uncle Ed as their guide.

Emma bent down to pick up a shiny slipper shell that a few minutes before had been covered by water. "We've seen high tide and low tide," she said. "But what causes the change of tides, Uncle Ed?"

"Well, by definition tides are the rise and fall of ocean waters on a regular time schedule. There is a constant tidal rhythm — high, low, high, low. This swing of the tides creates the seashore, an area that belongs first to the sea, then to the land.

Ocean tides are caused chiefly by the moon's attraction on the waters of the earth. The moon actually pulls the waters towards itself. Although all bodies of water are subject to tide producing forces it is only where large land masses and large bodies of water, like continents and oceans, come together that tides are great enough to be noticed.

There I go sounding like a professor again. You are going to have to forgive me if I do that too often. I've spent so much time in the classroom that it just comes naturally.

But if I haven't made something clear, don't hesitate to ask questions. Questions are good —all questions. If my students didn't have a few questions for me after a class, I felt that I hadn't stimulated their minds enough. So, ask your questions."

"Last summer we went to the Great Lakes but I didn't notice any tides. Do lakes have tides?" I asked.

"Yes, they do," answered Uncle Ed, "but you most likely wouldn't see that tide. In the inland bodies of water, the rise and fall is small. It probably wouldn't be noticed because of the action of wind and weather that also causes changes in the water level.

Lake Superior, one of the Great Lakes, has a tide with a range of only two inches. But the ocean is BIG and does things in a BIG way. Ocean tides can range up to 50 ft."

"Does everyplace have the same number of tides a day?" questioned Emma.

"No, they don't. The Atlantic Ocean has tides regularly twice a day but some places have only one daily tide. It depends on many things, the formation of the seacoast itself as well as the shape, size and depth of the water. Many things make a difference in the action of the tide."

"I think I read somewhere that the high tide is higher when the moon is full," I said.

"That's just about right, Ryan. It's immediately after a full moon or a new moon that the high tide is higher, and the low tide is lower. This is called a spring tide. The word spring doesn't mean a season but a fullness of the water, which might be said to 'spring'.

Do either of you know the name given the lower tides when the moon is in its first and third quarters?"

"I know it's a funny word, but I've forgotten it," volunteered Emma.

"That funny word is neaps. The word neaps goes back to a Scandinavian word meaning 'hardly enough'. Tides at this time do not get as high, or as low, as they do during the spring tides.

The tides are very important. In fact, in many places the tide is more important to the people than the clock. For instance, to the fisherman who needs high water to leave or reach his harbor, it is the morning and evening whistle, the beginning and ending of his working day. Each day as the time of the high tide changes he must change his schedule by about fifty minutes."

A group of sandpipers caught our attention and we stopped to watch their search for breakfast. "Sometimes the beach appears lifeless and empty to someone who doesn't know where to look," said Uncle Ed. "But the sandpipers know. Their long bills are probing into the low tide homes of mole crabs, and finding a tasty meal.

Beneath our feet many other sea animals have burrowed against the heat of the sun and the appetites of their enemy. They are waiting the return of the high tide and a chance to be more active again. We are like giants walking across the rooftops of an underground city."

We studied the sandpipers. Their actions followed the rhythm of the retreating waves. First, they chased the gentle wave toward the sea as it uncovered a tasty bit of food. Then the incoming wave chased them, its foam swirling around their legs.

Again and again, the little birds repeated their ritual, probing, prying with their long beaks into the wet sand. We stood spellbound by their actions, as in and out of waves they went. The water came ever so close but never quite reached their plump bodies.

Breaking the spell Uncle Ed said, "I'm getting hungry how about you two?" We started jogging along the wet sand and back to the cottage.

Emma stopped short .in front of the driftwood sign as we neared the front door. A little hesitantly, "Uncle Ed, you said we should ask questions. Well, I felt a little dumb for not knowing the answer — but what does 'Spindrift' mean?"

With a twinkle in his eye Uncle Ed said, "I was wondering when you would ask that. Many grownups aren't familiar with that word either. You could ask Google but look it up in the dictionary while I start breakfast."

A well-worn dictionary sat on Uncle Ed's desk. We thumbed through it until — spindrift — spray blown from a rough sea or surf.

"That's a perfect name," I said, "It's a lively word, a word that shows motion and change. It's a name you'd only find at the ocean. I didn't know what spindrift meant either but I thought you'd think I was stupid. I won't be afraid to ask a question next time."

"Good," laughed Uncle Ed. "Let's have a motto here. When you don't know — ask. "Agreed?"

"Agreed," Emma and I said with a smile.

"How about the message you promised your parents?" asked Uncle Ed.

"We'll do it right away," I promised. Enthusiasm and Uncle Ed's computer quickly sent our parents a lively update and we were ready to eat.

The walk had sharpened our appetites and Uncle Ed's delicious breakfast was soon only a memory. Working together the dishes were quickly washed and back in the cupboard. Now we were ready for the day's activities.

Uncle Ed had a suggestion. "If you feel energetic today, we can walk farther up the beach to an area of large sand dunes. It's a long walk, though."

"Of course, we feel energetic," I said, eager to leave.

"Then we'll go to the dunes," said Uncle Ed. "But don't forget your sun shirts and wide brimmed hats and sneakers. We'll be out in the sun most of the day and sunburn can ruin a beach visit."

We packed a lunch, grabbed our sun protection, and were on our way.

We headed north along the water's edge. We hadn't gone in this direction before and every step was new. Beach houses became fewer and fewer; soon there were none.

Although we had started out walking side by side, we didn't stay that way for long. One or the other was always stopping, stooping, examining something new and calling the others back to share another curiosity. Our long walk became longer, but more fun. We walked along with eyes ever downcast, searching the shifting sands.

My pockets already jingled with additions to my beach glass collection. I had found an especially interesting piece today, and the day was still young.

Emma darted into a retreating wave trying to snatch a shell that had caught her eye. It had vanished. She waited for a few more waves hoping to see her shell again but then continued walking. "Oh, well," she sighed, "I'll find another one later."

Up ahead was a large dark object lying at the water's edge. Something was moving. It was alive, and we ran toward it.

A horseshoe crab had been washed ashore and was lying on its back, waving its legs, desperately trying to turn over. "We'll give this gal a chance to right herself and help her if she can't," said Uncle Ed.

We watched in fascination as the crab worked to get its tail into the sand. We could feel the great effort it took, but then success. The crab pushed itself over and waddled back into the water. Emma and I continued along imitating the crab's funny walk. Up, down, up, down.

"How did you know the crab was a girl?" I asked.

"It was an educated guess, Ryan," said Uncle Ed. "Female horseshoe crabs are larger and broader than the males. Some people call them King crabs but they aren't related to crabs at all. These strange creatures are more closely related to the spiders. Their ancestors were around more than 450 million years ago -- a fact hard to imagine.

They usually come onto the shore only to lay their eggs. Although their egg laying season has passed -one occasionally does come ashore, as you just saw. They look a little frightening, but they are harmless to humans.

The horseshoe crab is vitally important to shore birds that migrate thousands of miles from South America to the Arctic and stop where horseshoe crabs lay millions of eggs each year. The eggs are like a superfood for these birds that need to refuel before flying north. For a long time, they weren't appreciated and were even ground up for fertilizer but now they are known to be really important in medicine too. Surprisingly their blood is blue and medical researchers are using properties in their blood as a protection from harmful bacteria. The crabs are returned to the ocean after donating some blood and it is very important that they are treated carefully so they survive for years to come.

The jellyfish you don't like to swim with are also helping scientists develop important medicines that may improve our brains. Research in the future will find other amazing secrets from our fascinating sea creatures.

I am happy to say that your cousin Becky is now a marine biologist and loves to share exciting new research with me. She recently told me about work in Brazil. Doctors are using specially treated skin from the Tilapia fish to help burn victims heal. There is still so much to learn from the sea and its creatures. Nature is amazing."

Looking again at the horseshoe crab, Emma said "their tails look like swords."

"That they do," agreed Uncle Ed. "Some people nicknamed them swordtails. The Native Americans who lived in this area long ago used the horseshoe crab tails for spears. They caught the crabs for food, too although I haven't tried one yet.

"We're almost to our destination. 'Steady as she goes'; as they say on the sea."

We had reached an area where sand dunes, stretching ahead as far as we could see, paralleled the shore. There were no signs of people; no one on the beach, no sounds of automobiles, no distant voices, no litter — all freshness.

Our footprints along the sand were the only signs of humans. We felt as if we had walked into another world, yet we knew it was only minutes from a bustling community.

For a few quiet moments we just sat, enjoying the peaceful surroundings. And then, as if by some unheard signal, we three got up and raced toward the inviting waters, breaking the silence with our laughter.

The cool water felt so refreshing after our long walk. We swam and splashed, splashed and swam. While Uncle Ed took a swim in deeper water Emma and I lay on an almost exposed sand bar, letting the foam swirl all around us. It was so restful.

A yell of sudden, sharp pain ended my rest. There dangling from my big toe was a crab. He seemed as surprised as I was, because he quickly released his hold and scampered across the sand. I laughed about it while telling Uncle Ed, but my toe still hurt. We played in the water a while longer; our constantly moving legs proved uninviting to other crabs. Then leaving the water we flopped down on our towels to let the warm sun dry our bodies. A lone, but noisy gull soon circled overhead, ending our nap.

"O.K., fellas, we hear you," called Uncle Ed. "But we don't have any scraps for you until after lunch. Come back later." And as if understanding, the gull flew farther down the beach, talking to himself.

"Let's take a look at this place," suggested Uncle Ed. "Can you see any differences in the dunes here compared to the ones by Spindrift?"

Emma quickly responded. "The dunes by your house look very different. They're higher; they sort of look like a wall."

"They are like a wall, Emma," said Uncle Ed. "They are called barrier dunes and are a very important way of preventing the water from flooding the lower areas behind it. I've been fortunate. The dune protecting my little house has withstood some fierce storms. Fortunately, dunes can rebuild."

"How do the dunes rebuild?" I asked.

"Dunes are made of very fine grains of sand that are carried by the wind," answered Uncle Ed. The sand is constantly being rearranged and no grain of sand remains long in one place. The dunes grow grain up again new sand is blown on top of that. on grain. A higher area is created on the side opposite the direction from which the wind comes. Have either of you ever heard of a 'travelling dune'?"

"No," we both answered.

"Sometimes a section of beach has lost its natural vegetation and the winds actually start to move it. The sand on the top is blown forward. The new top sand is blown on top of that, and again new sand is blown on top of that. This in effect causes the dune to move forward. Depending on conditions, dunes have been known to move as much as forty feet a year."

"Wow!" Emma and I said in unison,

"We'll need sneakers to explore the dunes because the sand is very hot. Let's take a look."

As we approached the dune Emma said, "It doesn't look like anything lives here. Is it as lifeless as it looks?"

"I think I know the answer," I boasted. "The sand is so hot that the things living here wait until it's cooler, maybe at night, to come out."

"Right, Ryan," said Uncle Ed, "although there are some mammals active in spite of the heat. They are mostly insects that can fly to higher, cooler air when the heat gets unbearable. It takes careful observation to locate some of the dune insects since many are sand colored."

"The sand sure is hot here," said Emma.

"I've stuck a thermometer into dune sand," said Uncle Ed, "and found it to be 120. degrees. A few inches farther down the temperature was 80. degrees. How else could dune life survive this heat if it was not able to fly to cooler air?"

"Maybe it has a fur coat, or something," volunteered Emma.

"Don't be a dummy," I laughed.

With a smile Uncle Ed said, "Emma is really correct, Ryan. All of the insect dune dwellers have a fur-like covering that either insulates them from the heat, or else it reflects the heat."

Feeling a little embarrassed, I said, "Sorry about the dummy bit, Emma. Next time I'll think first."

"That's O.K. It was a lucky guess," said Emma.

"Boy, I can feel the heat right through my sneakers," I complained.

"Before we go back to the cooler sands, let's look closely for signs of life," suggested Uncle Ed.

"I see some holes over there," called Emma.

"And some funny tracks, too," I added.

"Just as we saw in other areas, first impressions aren't always accurate," said Uncle Ed. "It takes a second, more careful look to notice many forms of life. Let's see if we can identify some of the tracks."

"Those look like some insects made them" I said. "But what made the track that looks like a path of holes?"

"Maybe we'll know if we follow them," said Uncle Ed.

We slowly traced the tracks until they ended at a round, deep hole. Bending down, Uncle Ed said, "Here's the home of a ghost crab. Too bad we can't see him. He can really scoot across the sand. But if we did have a chance to see him, you'd know how he got his name. While standing still, the ghost crab's coloration blends so well with the sand that he seems to disappear right before your eyes."

"Uncle Ed," called Emma excitedly. "What made that funny track? It looks like a braid."

"Good girl, Emma, said Uncle Ed. "You've found the trail of a hognose snake. He's a harmless fellow but he puffs and hisses if provoked. Snakes usually wait for night to move about so we probably won't see him either."

We watched in fascination as a gentle breeze blew a bent blade of marram grass. It etched a perfect circle in the sand The wind was quite an artist. We fried to imitate the smooth lines formed by the wind, but failed.

Starting back toward the water Uncle Ed continued, "At night there is much activity on the dunes. I have seen toads, lizards, rabbits, spiders and even bats in this area at night. You're probably ready for another swim after the heat of the dunes."

"I'm glad I don't have to live in such a hot place," I said.

Lunch was followed by a lazy afternoon spent probing, plowing and playing in the sand. At the water's edge we caught mole crabs. These were the crabs that we had seen the sandpipers eating. The mole crabs, or beach bugs as some people call them, are fat, oval shaped crabs, unlike other crabs we had seen.

There were dozens of them on every retreating wave, but you had to be quick to catch one. When we did catch one, we gently placed it on the sand at the water's edge and watched as they vanished, almost as if they had been swallowed by the sand. Two paddle like legs helped them to dig into the sand but the speed was amazing. Over and over, we caught, and then freed, the mole crabs never tiring of watching them vanish faster than we could say their name.

The moving sun and our complaining stomachs told us that it was time to return to port in this case Spindrift.

As we headed back along the beach, Uncle Ed shared an important memory about a hard time at Spindrift. "Many years ago, when my girls were very young, a violent hurricane named Ben, caused tremendous damage in this area. Everyone evacuated inland for safety and it was a week before we were allowed to return.

News broadcasts had shown terrible damage all along the coast and many miles inland. We didn't know what to expect. Would Spindrift still be there and what about our neighbors?

As we headed back to the beach, we passed many areas of damage and destruction. When we approached town, we saw the water tower knocked almost to the ground. Then we came to the small bridge that had been across the marsh. It had been washed away. The State workers had quickly put up a temporary one lane bridge that was now four times wider than the old bridge and now crossed over a flowing stream of water.

We were getting nervous. What had happened? What were we going to find?

We pulled into Sandpiper Lane and stopped in amazement. We saw lots of debris and damage. There was sand piled everywhere but the houses all seemed to have survived. But something was different.

When we reached Spindrift and got out of the car our amazement turned to awe. The storm had cut a channel just past our community that now connected the bay to the ocean.

Huge mounds of sand had piled on top of our barrier dunes and made them higher and safer. The channel now separated us from the beach that we used to walk to town. But the dunes had saved our community.

As neighbors returned, we all gathered to check out the damage and count our blessings. We spontaneously agreed to change Sandpiper Lane to Lucky Lane. It is a constant reminder of the power of hurricanes.

The neighbors enthusiastically formed the Lucky Lane Gang We located the homes needing immediate help and went to work.

In the morning, many friends and family, including your dad and two of his friends came to join the cleanup crew. .1n twenty-four hours we had all the urgent repairs done. We then went into town to offer help wherever it was needed. We joined many other volunteers who came to help.

It was many weeks, even months before the area recovered, but working together we had done wonders. It took months for the permanent bridge to be completed and the water tower to be restored.

There is a large display of photographs of the hurricane in the community center which we can visit before you leave. I think there is even a picture of your Dad and his friends.

We had taken good care of our barrier dunes before the hurricane but now we needed to plant the larger dunes.

Volunteers from the Nature Center came with dune grasses. They trained neighbors, including children your ages to plant and care for the dunes. The dunes had saved our community and we really value and appreciate them.

Our Dune Grass Gang is still looking after our dunes and helping others to restore and care for their dunes.

Years later our Lucky Lane Gang is also still helping when needed to keep our town and area safe."

We could see the Lucky Lane community ahead. We were very grateful that it had survived and thrived all those years ago.

It was good to be in the comfortable coziness of Spindrift again. We were tired, happy and hungry and while we ate, we reviewed some of the things that we had found so interesting.

"I've been wondering about tides," I said, "where does all the high tide water go when it is low tide?"

"Good question," said Uncle Ed, reaching for a pen and pad. As he talked the words took on additional meaning in a simple sketch on the paper.

"Here we have the earth and its vast oceans. Three quarters of the earth is water, which is a lot of water. The moon acts on the earth's waters like a big magnet and pulls on these waters making bulges around the center of the earth.

As the moon travels around the earth, the bulge follows making high tide. This happens because the earth is slowly turning around once a day, the tidal bulge is staying in line with the moon, while the oceans are moving with the turning earth.

The bulge on the side of the earth facing the moon is matched by another bulge on the opposite side. These are the tides that follow the moon's path around the earth, which takes about 24 hours.

"What effect does the sun have on the tides?" Emma asked.

"Although the sun also pulls at the earth's waters the effect is less than the moon's because of its great distance from the earth," said Uncle Ed. "But after the full moon, and again after the new moon, the sun and moon are directly in line with the earth and they pull together. Then we have ...

"Spring tide," Emma and I chorused.

"I think you're getting the idea," laughed Uncle Ed. "I hope you understand today's lesson because I'm going to give you a test on the tides tomorrow."

We knew from his grin that he was only kidding but we wanted to understand it, test or no test. We studied the sketch and the confusion in our minds about tides lessened. "I think I'm getting the idea, too," I said.

We had been so involved in the discussion that we failed to see the sun nearing the horizon. The kitchen was suddenly lighted with a rosy glow as if the sun was saying get ready to enjoy my nightly show.

We sat enchanted as the sun settled down for the night, leaving the sky and clouds streaked with every shade of pink and red.

It was a very peaceful moment. I looked at Emma. We hadn't had a squabble in over 24 hours. In fact, she had been fun to have around. I wondered if this special place had something to do with the new way I felt.

Uncle Ed looked at me knowingly, "Sunsets are one of my favorite things, especially when they go down on a day well spent.

"Tomorrow will be another busy day. Time for bed now so you will be ready for it."

****

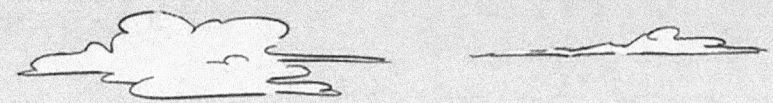

Day Three

"Time to get up, sleepyheads," coaxed Uncle Ed. "We've got a date with the low tide and it waits for no one."

For a few sleepy seconds I looked around trying to remember where I was. Low tide! Today we were going to see the tidal pools.

I jumped out of bed calling to Emma, "Get up. The tide won't wait for us."

In record time we were dressed and at the breakfast table. "Whoa!" cautioned Uncle Ed. "No need to rush so. We've still got time to enjoy our meal. And for lunch — how would you like to stop at a restaurant in town?"

"Oh, boy!" Emma and I said in unison.

Soon we were headed south in Uncle Ed's car, away from the familiar toward the new. "You know we are going to the tidal pools, but do you know what a tidal pool is?" questioned Uncle Ed.

For a few seconds neither of us spoke. Then Emma said, "If we have to be there when the tide is low, I guess it's a pool that you can only see when the tide is out."

"Good guess," said Uncle Ed. "Sometimes pools are created on our sand beach at low tide but they are not the same, as we shall see."

Before long the road edged nearer the water and we caught sight of a different kind of shoreline. Instead of the wide sand beaches there were huge rocks and boulders. We could hardly wait to explore!

"Ryan, what do you think we might find in a tidal pool?" asked Uncle Ed.

"Well," I said hesitantly, "probably some small things, like starfish and snails and little fish. Nothing big like a horseshoe crab."

"We'll soon see if you're correct," said Uncle Ed as he parked the car on a siding by the road. "We are fortunate that today is cloudy. On a bright day the pool dwellers can be seen more easily by the birds and other enemies and are forced to hide. But hopefully they won't be hiding today. Does this look the way you expected?"

"I didn't know what to expect," said Emma, "but this looks great."

"Before we go down to the pools, let me give you a few words of warning," said Uncle Ed. "This area can be very dangerous. The rocks are slippery and should be walked across cautiously — no running. And we must be alert for the incoming tide. If we are not watchful, the tide can strand us among the rocks which will be a bad situation, to say the least.

"Don't look so worried. It can be lots of fun if we respect this special area. Take a good look at the rocks from up here first. Do you see anything?" challenged Uncle Ed.

"Do you mean the stripes along the rocks?" I asked.

"That's what I was hoping you'd see," said Uncle Ed. "They are often called bands or zones."

"What causes the stripes?" asked Emma.

"Let's go down and see," said Uncle Ed. "First we'll look at the pools and then check the bands. You two follow me. When I see a likely spot to stop, we'll approach it quietly, and try not to make the pool inhabitants aware of our presence."

Cautiously, we started making our way down the rocky slope. The rocks seemed to be heaped in great confusion and disorder. The first few feet went well and I wondered about Uncle Ed's warning. It looked like an easy jump to the next rock, so I jumped, slipped and landed hard.

Uncle Ed gave me a knowing look and asked, "You O.K., Ryan?"

"Sure, sure," I said, continuing with more care. Now I could see the reason for the warning. The rocks were covered with a blackish growth that was like a slippery carpet.

With a wave of his arm, Uncle Ed motioned for us to crouch down. We stretched out on this carpet that helped to cushion us from the hard rock. The edge of the pool was lined with seaweed, hanging heavy in the still water.

Cautiously, expectantly we inched toward the edge and peered into the tidal pool. What we saw was a magical, miniature world of the sea.

This little community was crowded with a great variety of life. We could see them interacting the way they do in the deeper waters, usually unseen.

The floor of the pool was lined with seaweeds and many empty shells. Searching through the pile of abandoned snail shells was a hermit crab in search of a new home. I thought that the shell he was wearing was very nice, but it didn't seem to please him anymore. He selected a new one, turned it over and passed it by; then another. But nothing seemed to be what he had in mind.

Just then he spied another hermit crab already wearing the shell he wanted. Boldly he approached the other crab and started a fight. We watched in fascination as the crabs poked and jabbed with their waving claws. Finally, the tired crab left his shell and hurried off into the sea weed. The victor proudly put on his new home and strutted off to show his neighbors.

Next, we saw a four-legged starfish tightly wrapped around a large blue mussel. Persistence paid off and the starfish forced the mussel open and got ready to enjoy a meal. Uncle Ed said our "starfish" was really a sea-star, since it isn't a fish. I'll probably still call it a starfish.

In the far corner was a group of beautiful pink sea anemones with waving flowerlike heads. Uncle Ed motioned for us to watch. Gently he dropped a small snail, called a periwinkle, over the waving tentacles of the anemone.

Like a flash it grabbed the snail and drew it into its mouth. Then suddenly it changed from a flowerlike creature to a plain looking lump on the bottom of the pool. After eating it would again bloom like a flower to await another unsuspecting creature that entered its territory.

Barnacles covered an area of rock and we could see them feeding. They were really alive! When exposed to the air, they closed up and looked lifeless, but now they showed their feathered legs, which first swept the water to gather plankton and then combed the food into their mouths. It was amazing!

A moving object caught my eye. For the first time I saw a live scallop with bright blue eyes edging its shell. While I watched in wonder, the scallop travelled through the water by flapping its shell open and closed. It looked like it was taking bites out of the water as it moved forward.

"It's almost time to move on," said Uncle Ed with obvious regret. "There are still other things to see and the tide is moving up. We'll want to examine the projecting rocks over there that show the bands so clearly."

Once we were close the bands seemed to blend together; the stripes no longer looked distinct. We had to look closely to see the life that had created these bands. Uncle Ed explained that the uppermost band, that appeared black, was really made of blue-green algae one of the earth's most ancient plants. This was the growth that made the rocks so slippery.

Below this were periwinkles which seemed to be grazing on the rock. The next band was white, made by barnacles crowded closely together. Their plates were all tightly closed; they awaited the return of the tide.

"This is the high tide line," explained Uncle Ed. "Notice how the barnacles fill almost every bit of the rock. But a few blue mussels have managed to establish small colony over there. " Under the barnacles hung brown masses of seaweeds.

"Do these seaweeds have a name?" I asked.

"This is the rockweed or wrack. It provides a good home for many forms of life. Below the rockweeds is another kind of seaweed called Irish Moss," said Uncle Ed, reaching below the water to grab a handful of reddish-brown plant. This is harvested in many areas and provides a substance called carrageenan that is used in some medicines, cosmetics and food products."

The water was now lapping around our ankles and we knew it was time to go. Reluctantly we said goodbye to the creatures of the tide pool who would soon be covered with surf. Our sneakers squished water as we began climbing.

"We'll talk more about the algae when we are safely above the water. Careful, now," cautioned Uncle Ed. "Remember it is …"

Splash! Uncle Ed had slipped and was knee deep in water. His hat sat comically in the middle of the pool.

When Uncle Ed began to laugh, Emma and I dared to join in. "I told you it was slippery," finished Uncle Ed, reaching for his hat.

But now his hat had a decoration. A starfish was stretched out on the brim, his suction feet holding on tightly. Uncle Ed gently, but firmly, pulled him off and returned him to the water.

We continued our climb until we were above the high tide line where we sat to rest and dry off. We watched the water inching up toward the pool that had so fascinated us and were grateful for the time, though brief, to enjoy this area.

A seagull circled the rocks, then dropped the clam shell he was carrying. The shell broke open and the clever gull quickly swooped down to enjoy his snack. He flew off to find another clam, leaving us alone.

No one talked for quite a while. We were hypnotized by the sight and sound of the foaming water licking at the rocks.

Uncle Ed was the first to speak. "Watching the incoming tide is a very captivating thing. I often lose all sense of time and mission, I become so involved with enjoying this great, but every day, event.

But let's talk a little more about the algae, lest I forget to mention them later. There are many uses for seaweeds, or algae. I mentioned Irish moss; an extract obtained from this plant is used to cure leather, make shoe polish as well as the uses I named before.

"Can you eat seaweeds?" I asked.

"Oh, yes," replied Uncle Ed. "They are very nutritious and are an important part of the diet in many parts of the world, especially Asian countries. Scientists are working now to make wider use of algae as a source of food.

I have some tasty seaweed snacks for tonight. Don't make such a funny face, Ryan. I think you will be pleasantly surprised."

Uncle Ed was right. The seaweed chips were really very tasty. I often buy different seaweeds now and surprise my Asian friends with my appreciation of them.

"1 remember reading about using seaweed as fertilizer," said Emma.

"That's right, Emma. After a storm many gardeners near the shore gather this valuable, but free, fertilizer.

"Algin is a substance also obtained from seaweed, the brown variety, which is used in dairy products, salad dressings, hair creams and cosmetics. The giant kelps, one of the brown algae also, provide the chemical iodine. And agar is obtained from red algae and used to culture bacteria in laboratories. Algae can also be used in meal to feed livestock."

"There's a lot more to seaweed than I thought," said Emma, thoughtfully.

"And I'm sure there will be more uses found in the future. It all goes back to one of my favorite themes. Man must learn to respect the sea, and with this respect will come an appreciation for all that the sea provides and nurtures.

It's a good feeling to watch the two of you develop this respect since it is your generation that will probably be faced with the greatest challenges to the wise use of this great natural resource — and besides, it has been fun having you visit." Uncle Ed gave us a smile that quietly said so much. We felt good all over.

We sat enjoying that feeling for a few minutes until my hunger forced me to say, "Uncle Ed, isn't it time to eat?"

"Yes, it is, Ryan," laughed Uncle Ed. "We don't need a clock when you are around to announce mealtime. Time to leave, I'm afraid."

With a last fond look, we climbed into the car and were on our way. We were soon back on the main road dotted with every variety of restaurant.

"Pizza, Uncle Ed. Let's have pizza," Emma and I called as we approached Sal's Pizza Parlor.

"It wasn't quite what I had in mind," said Uncle Ed, "but if that's what you'd like, that's what we'll have."

The aroma of cheese and tomatoes greeted us as we entered. We were soon devouring a hot, tasty, pizza. "Your ability to consume food amazes me," said Uncle Ed with a laugh. "I'd forgotten how much growing children eat. I haven't had pizza in a long time. I'm glad you suggested it." Emma and I were glad too.

"It's discouraging," I said, "to forget the names of all the interesting things we've seen. It really makes me feel dumb."

"Cheer up, Ryan," laughed Uncle Ed. "You have lots of company. It's nice to be able to remember the names but it is impossible to know them all. The important thing is to enjoy them."

"Do you have trouble remembering names, Uncle Ed?" asked Emma in amazement. "You seem to know everything."

"Then let me make a confession. I can't remember the names of ordinary garden flowers, but I know the wildflowers. It really used to bother your Aunt Barbara who had a beautiful garden. I know many birds on sight but can't identify many of their calls, and I'd like to. So don't worry about the names, they aren't that important. I love dahlias even if I call them daisies and that's what counts."

"That makes me feel better," I said with a smile. We carefully divided up the last piece of pizza. Appetites satisfied we climbed back into the car. It was only a short ride to the road that led to the bird sanctuary, the second stop on our trip.

A narrow road wound between low bushes and dwarf trees until we passed a pond carpeted with water lilies. Ahead was the wildlife refuge, its gate opening onto vast stretches of marshland.

Uncle Ed was parking the car when a man standing nearby called, "Ed! It's good to see you. Who are your friends?"

"I'm glad you're here today, Tom," said Uncle Ed "I'd like you to meet my brother's children, Emma and Ryan. Mr. Butler is the superintendent of the sanctuary. We've been friends for a long time."

"I always enjoy having your uncle visit," said Mr. Butler "He is always so enthusiastic and interested in all that is new. And we've had a new addition since you were last here, but I'm afraid it's not the kind I like to boast about. Come and I'll show you."

We headed toward the marshes bordered by soft reeds and cattails. Mr. Butler talked as we walked toward our destination. "This is the quiet season at the refuge. At peak migration times we have over 100,000 birds. They stay for varying lengths of time and attract many people to view them."

We could hear the birds quacking and honking before we saw them. A wire fence formed a large pen which seemed a strange thing in a place like this. But then we saw the reason.

A group of ducks and geese were gathered together, looking very bedraggled and sad. "This," said Mr. Butler, "is where we must keep the survivors of a recent oil spill.

These fellows were luckier than many others, but until they are stronger and have grown some new feathers, we will care for them.

"The cleaning agents that had to be used removed much of the natural coating on the feathers of the birds that enables them to float. They couldn't survive if left on their own."

"I feel so sorry for them," said Emma sadly.

"Hopefully they will be able to leave soon," said Mr. Butler. "They don't like being confined. We have to keep them away from the visitor area so that we don't encourage sympathetic people making pets of them. It wouldn't be wise for them to have too much human contact if they are to return to a wild state."

We turned back toward the main sanctuary, the sound of the confined birds echoing in our ears. "You're invited to start your tour in my office," offered Mr. Butler. There are some interesting photos that I think you will like."

"I was hoping you'd extend that invitation, Tom," said Uncle Ed with a smile.

The walls of the office were completely covered with pictures of birds. All had been photographed locally and were grouped according to season. Glancing around I said, "That sure is a lot of birds. How many different kinds of birds live here?"

"More than 250 kinds of birds have been officially identified here," answered Mr. Butler, "But some have only been seen a few times."

"How many kinds of birds are there?" questioned Emma.

"Well, Emma," said Mr. Butler, "in the world there are about 10,000 kinds of birds. In all of North America there are about 1,700 kinds. If you exclude Mexico and Central America there are about 730 kinds."

"I didn't know there were so many kinds," I said thoughtfully. "Do you know if anyone has ever seen all the kinds of birds there are in North America?"

"Not that I know of, Ryan," answered Mr. Butler. "But I know people who have seen over 600 different kinds of birds. Many serious bird watchers have 'life lists' of 500 or more kinds. And it wouldn't be unusual for an amateur to identify 300 kinds."

"But remember that numbers are not the important thing. Enjoying while studying the bird's environment and habits is better than mere numbers. Bird watching isn't isolated from the enjoyment of other forms of nature and is a very rewarding interest."

"My secretary has just reminded me of an appointment. I'm sorry I can't spend more time with you, children. Enjoy your visit today and I hope you'll come again during our busy migration and nesting seasons."

We said goodbye to Mr. Butler and continued examining the pictures. There were many birds I knew or heard of, like heron, mallard, snow goose, hawk, osprey, tern, woodpecker, chickadee, nuthatch, sparrow, and goldfinch.

But there were many names that were new to me, and I made a list so that I could read about them later — dowitchers, phalaropes, kestrels, oystercatchers, vireos, turnstones, whimbrels, and shearwaters.

Looking at a picture that showed the sky darkened by a huge flock of Canada geese Uncle Ed said, "This refuge is a part of the Atlantic Flyway, which is a corridor or pathway for birds during their migration. The sanctuary provides a resting place with abundant food and nesting areas for many kinds of birds that migrate from north to south in winter and south to north in spring. This picture shows very well what Mr. Butler meant by the busy season.

Sometimes the wetlands and marshes are thought of as wastelands by people who don't understand their importance. But they are a very necessary part of the total environment."

We continued to examine the wall, finding some pictures amazing, comical, majestic and unbelievable. One set of pictures showed in series the arrival of some oil-soaked birds, their bodies covered with black ooze. We saw the cleaning they had to undergo and later their return to nature.

"Let's go and see what birds we can find," suggested Emma,

"I was about to suggest that myself," said Uncle Ed. "We'll have to share field glasses but if you're ready let us be on our way. There is an auto route through the marshes. We can stop along it whenever you'd like."

Back in the car we drove very slowly, calling excitedly whenever a new bird was sighted. Field glasses were constantly being passed around to allow a closer look. Without the glasses we would have missed many birds as well as a close look at their colors and feeding habits.

Majestic looking egrets stalked the marshes on long legs. A family of Canada geese slid by in perfect formation without even rippling the still water. Other geese flapped their great wings in an impressive five-foot expanse.

At the observation tower we climbed to see a panoramic view across the wide stretches of marsh. Birds were everywhere. The air was filled to overflowing with their songs and calls.

"Try to imagine," said Uncle Ed, "this area totally filled with birds. It's quite a sight—and sound."

"I'd like to come then to see them," said Emma.

"Me, too," I added.

"Consider yourselves invited then — and bring your parents along. We can make it a nice weekend visit."

We continued our trip leisurely, stopping often. Swallows and red-winged blackbirds darted everywhere. They were so free and happy here.

I was sorry to see the road exit by Mr. Butler's office. We could see him at the window; we waved and headed back to Spindrift.

All was quiet for a few minutes. "Something seems to be bothering the two of you," said Uncle Ed knowingly.

"I keep thinking of the birds behind that fence," said Emma.

"I hope it doesn't happen again," I said.

"I wish I felt confident that it wouldn't happen again, but it probably will,' said Uncle Ed. "We feel sorry for the birds, and we should, since they are innocent victims. But we should remember that less noticeable things are damaged or killed whenever we see injured birds.

The oil can destroy whole food chains. Man has a bad habit of thinking, or forgetting, that even though the spilled oil is out of sight, maybe at the bottom of the ocean, it continues to cause harm for a long time."

"What can be done about it?" I asked.

"I wish I had a simple answer, Ryan," said Uncle Ed, "but it is a complex problem. There is always the chance of an accident happening but more must be done to decrease these chances. As much research and enthusiasm should be used to develop efficient ways of recovering spilled oil as is used to develop the facilities that produce oil. And then those involved have to be vigilant enough to look deeply and completely when oil spills occur. Dead birds and fish are only part of the problem.

I'm sure a solution can be found, but it's going to take more effort than has been used. I think it is possible to have oil and a safeguarded environment. It just has to be.

The two of you can't solve the problem now by worrying about it so how about some smiles; that's better."

Suddenly I remembered the hurricane pictures at the community center. "Uncle Ed, can we stop to see the hurricane pictures?" I asked excitedly.\

"Let's do that " said Uncle Ed. "The community center is open when the Post Office is open so we have time to stop."

Behind the Post Office was a comfortable room with a stack of chairs along one wall, a small kitchen and lots and lots of pictures lining the remaining walls.

Many showed the town years ago, even before cars were common. Then we saw all the pictures of storms. Over the years the town had survived many storms. The pictures showed scenes of great damage and destruction.

But then we came to the most violent storm they had ever experienced. Hurricane Ben! The pictures were frightening even to see so many years later.

And then we saw them. The Lucky Lane Gang! There was our younger Dad, Uncle Ed and many neighbors looking tired, but determined. They had done so much to help the town. Underneath the picture was a plaque thanking them for all they had done to help the town survive. I felt very proud of them too.

We slowly looked at the sad pictures. But when we left and looked around at Main Street both Emma and I felt so grateful that this friendly town survived Hurricane Ben.

We were soon back at Spindrift. "I think," said Uncle Ed studying the sky, "that we'll delay dinner and take a swim now. We're going to see a storm before morning. Better enjoy the beach while we can.

We enjoyed a quick swim and then went back to Spindrift to share dinner and some talk of weather. "Why do you feel so sure we're going to have a storm?" I asked.

"I've been reading the weather," answered Uncle Ed. "When I was in college, I spent two summers working on a boat with a very weather-wise sea captain. He had spent years developing a knowledge of winds, clouds, the sea and animals, as they related to weather. He was a fascinating person to know.

"I'm not able to predict weather as accurately as he could but it's fun to try."

"I saw lots of clouds in the sky," said Emma, "But that doesn't always mean rain."

"That's right, Emma," said Uncle Ed. "It's a combination of different things that determines the weather. Clouds alone don't tell you enough."

"What kind of things told you that it would storm tomorrow?" I asked.

"The birds, for one thing," answered Uncle Ed. "The air thins before a storm, in other words there is less air pressure, and birds find it more difficult to fly then.

So, an absence of birds, or birds flying at a lower altitude, where the pressure is the greatest, is an accurate indication of a lowering barometer. And a lowering barometer means bad weather. The swallows were flying exceptionally low. There were few gulls, most had probably gone over to the bay area. The gulls I did see were roosting, with their backs to the wind.

The wind is a very important factor in the making of weather. The wind had changed from its fair-weather direction to one that usually means rain."

"The sunset didn't look red tonight," I added. "Does that mean anything?"

"Yes, it does, Ryan," said Uncle Ed. "You know the old saying:

> Red sky in the morning is a sailor's sure warning;
> Red sky at night is the sailor's delight.

Sailors often say that they can smell a storm coming," Those familiar with the sea can sense a stronger smell from the water. The smell of the marine plankton and other life in the sea is more obvious when the air thins as it does before a storm. The high pressure of fair weather holds in the smell normally. I've gotten fairly good at smelling a storm myself, if you'll allow me to boast a bit.

We all complain that the flies are in a biting mood before a rain. And did you notice how clearly we could hear that boat horn when we were down on the beach? The clouds were acting as a sounding board making the boat horn unusually clear. Of course, the old reliable weather forecasters are my aching joints. They can always predict a storm."

"I'm going to try to become weather-wise by watching for weather signs." I said. "Then I can be my own weatherman."

"Right you are, Ryan," agreed Uncle Ed. "But now it's time for bed. It's been a long and busy day. We'll see how good a weatherman I am in the morning."

Day Four

A loud rumble of thunder was the first thing I heard. The bedroom was very dark, too dark to see; I could only listen. Rain was pounding on the window. Waves crashed against the beach. A fog horn moaned in the wet blackness outside.

Uncle Ed was right about the weather forecast. But why did it have to rain and ruin our visit I rolled over and tried not to think about the storm, but it was hard to ignore the thundering, pounding, crashing sounds of the storm. I wrapped the blanket close around my ears and hoped that would help.

It was morning when I again woke up. The room was gloomy, reflecting the dark, dreary day. Emma was also just waking.

"Did you hear it?" I asked grumpily. "It thundered and rained all night. And it's still raining! Our day is ruined!"

Uncle Ed appeared in the doorway. "What's the problem, Ryan?" he asked. "You sound angry."

"The rain!" I said . "It's going to ruin our day. Why couldn't it wait until next week?"

"Suppose I promised you that your day wouldn't be ruined because of the rain, would you feel better?" asked Uncle Ed.

"I guess so," I said. "But how can you be so sure?"

"Remember when I told you that the beach had moods?" asked Uncle Ed. "Well, a rainy day at the beach is just one of nature's moods. I rather look forward to a rainy day, especially if I've been very busy. It's a good day for resting — and everyone and everything seems to do just that when it rains here.

"The storm won't last much longer; the clouds are now low and quick. The sun will be back and we'll be busy again. So, let's use this day for resting and catching up with some of the things we haven't had time to talk about.

"A good breakfast will make you feel a little better, I'm sure. So, smile, wash up and let's eat."

By the time I sat down to eat I was smiling and looking forward to the meal.

"This is a good day," said Uncle Ed, 'to talk about one of my favorite subjects water."

"You did talk about it," I interrupted.

"Some things about water were discussed," continued Uncle Ed, "but we could spend a week of rainy days talking about all the fascinating facts concerning water."

Emma made a face. "I know what you're thinking," said Uncle Ed. "Trust you old uncle. I told you it will clear today and it will.

I want to tell you a little about one of my favorite water subjects, the hydrologic cycle."

"The what?" I asked, not understanding.

"The hydrologic, or water cycle," repeated Uncle Ed.

"Oh, the water cycle," I said. "That's when the sun absorbs the water from the earth, it rains and the water comes back to earth again. It keeps going around.'"

"Maybe you already know what I intended to tell you," said Uncle Ed.

"I don't think so," I said, "Because that's all I know about it."

"Well, that's a good start, Ryan," said Uncle Ed. "But one fact that always amazes me is that the water in the oceans, the water raining on the roof, the water that grew your breakfast food, all water is the same water that has been around since the earth was made."

"I never thought of it that way before," said Emma.

"The water is always being recycled, reused," said Uncle Ed. "The rain falling now has probably fallen on dinosaurs and prehistoric man.

"Recall that three quarters of the earth is water. We couldn't live without water or the sun; it is the sun that evaporates the water into clouds which redistributes the water to the land.

Let me illustrate with one of my little sketches. Keep in mind when I say water, I mean water in all its forms, solid, liquid, gas; ice, hail, snow, rain, water vapor, fog.

The land absorbs some of the rain that falls and some runs off into streams and rivers. All of the water, whether it winds up in the leaves of a tree or an underground river eventually finds its way back to the oceans and the cycle repeats itself.

A drop of water might get evaporated even in the process of falling as rain or it might get absorbed underground and spend a thousand years before it is recycled again."

"So that's the hydrologic cycle," I said. "I've learned another new word. And I feel better. That was a good breakfast."

"Thanks, Ryan," said Uncle Ed. "The cook always appreciates a compliment."

"Uncle Ed, is it O.K. if I sweep the floors?" asked Emma. "They're very sandy."

"That's a good idea, Emma, and a thoughtful one," said Uncle Ed. "Sand is a fact of life in beach living and is constantly underfoot, and in clothes, in beds, in hair, in ears, everywhere. Some people never get used to living with and can't fully enjoy the beach."

While Emma swept, Uncle Ed and I cleaned up the dishes and chatted. I was beginning to feel that the rain, rather than confining me, was reminding me of the coziness that Spindrift and special friends offered. It was going to be a nice day in spite of the rain.

Emma appeared, broom in hand. "Uncle Ed, I was just wondering, where does sand come from? I noticed that it's not all the same color or size either."

"Think, Emma," said Uncle Ed. "You've seen the beach, the waves and the water. You tell me, where does sand come from?"

"The rocks and shells. The waves grind them up and make sand," answered Emma brightly.

"You knew the answer all along," said Uncle Ed. "Most of the sand on the beach was made long ago and continues to be made by the grinding action of the waves.

We don't know the age of our beach sand but some of it has probably been around since the first sand was made, long ago when the earth was young.

Over the ages rocks have been carried to the sea by rivers. Much of the sand in North America comes from the erosion of quartz rock, but mixed with this are grains of many other types of rocks, often garnet."

"I've heard of red sand," I said, "What other colors are sand?"

"Although garnet is red, it isn't the reason for real red sand, which comes from the erosion of red sandstone," said Uncle Ed. "But sand can be pink, black, gray, white, even green. It all depends on what formed the sand grains.

There is an abundance of sand along the continental shelf, which is a flooded, nearly flat extension of the continents. This sand is brought up and deposited on the beaches by the action of waves and currents."

"But don't shells make sand?" questioned Emma.

"I was coming to that, Emma," laughed Uncle Ed. "In many areas the sands are mostly shell material and are very white. We can almost watch the waves making sand out of our shells on the beach. They break down faster than rock.

That beach glass you are so fond of, Ryan, is in the process of becoming sand, too. Sand is a part of all glass and the waves are remaking sand of the beach glass — unless you get there first, of course, Ryan.

We often think of rock as being so durable and hard. But think of sand and you know that isn't true. It takes a long, long time but even the hardest rock wears away until it is the size of a grain of sand.

But sand is special — it is almost indestructible. It is the hard core that remains after all the grinding and polishing by the waves.

"Can you think of something that is useful because of just that indestructible property of sand?"

All was quiet and then I remembered. "Sandpaper!" I yelled.

"Your enthusiasm overwhelms me, Ryan," laughed Uncle Ed. "Sandpaper is right. So, the next time that sharp grain of sand scratches your sunburn while you are trying to sleep, think of it as an ancient and beautiful property of the beach. It might help."

"Uncle Ed, we haven't talked about waves," I said. "What causes waves?"

"I'm glad you reminded me," said Uncle Ed. "Waves should have been at the top of our discussion list.

The origin of waves is the same thing that controls so much of earth's activities, the sun. Out over the oceans the heat of the sun generates currents in the atmosphere. These winds cause friction with the surface of the sea.

The sea then absorbs some of this energy and waves develop. The force of the wind has less effect on the size of a wave than the distance over which the wind has blown. The farther the wind blows across the water the larger the wave.

We should have talked about this on the beach but you have watched the shore birds riding on the water. You know how they just bob up and down on the water. The water doesn't move them forward, just up and down, as the waves pass by. The same is true of other floating objects.

This is possible because only the force of the wave moves, the water itself doesn't move. The force merely moves through the water."

"But Uncle Ed," I interrupted, "how come we get knocked around so much when we're in the waves?"

"The two of you are always ahead of me," laughed Uncle Ed. "As the shoreline slopes the force is compressed and squeezed and then the water and the force move, as you know from playing in the waves.

The winds from last night's storm will leave us higher waves for a day or so and will deposit more debris, or treasure as I call it, on the beach today. Just wait and see."

"I've been waiting for one of you to remind me of lunch. I'm starving, how about you?"

"Let's eat," I said and we all laughed.

"First, let me start a fire in the fireplace," said Uncle Ed. "A brief one is all we'll need to chase away the dampness. And then we can pop some popcorn. How does that sound? No need to answer, your smiles tell it all.

After a storm is a good time to collect the driftwood that supplies my fireplace. Trouble is I find so much of it too attractive to burn. That pile in back that you were poking through the other day is the leftovers that I can't use and can't bear to destroy.

Sometimes I give a very choice piece as a gift and when I have visitors who can't find their own on the beach, they have my 'wood pile' to browse through. You can't beat Nature's art work when it comes to driftwood."

The fire was crackling now, its heat radiating across the room. "Today's a good day for soup and sandwich. Is that menu all right with you?"

"Sure is," I said enthusiastically.

We ate slowly, enjoying the warmth of the fire, the warmth of the company.

"I'm always glad for an excuse for a fire and popcorn," said Uncle Ed as he prepared the popper. "How about a game of Monopoly while we wait for the storm to pass?"

"I'd like that," said Emma.

"That sounds like fun," I agreed.

The fire was just right for popping corn and the kernels were soon swelling, bursting and bouncing around the wire cage. They smelled so good and tasted even better.

"I have an electric corn popper," said Uncle Ed, "but it somehow tastes better fixed this way."

Our mouths were too stuffed to answer, we just shook our heads in agreement.

"Let's pop another batch for later. I'll probably have to hide it or it will never last," said Uncle Ed with a laugh.

So, the afternoon slid by; Monopoly and popcorn. I really didn't care if it stopped raining or not. The game never quite ended. It was obvious that Uncle Ed had soundly beaten us and we conceded defeat with just a few dollars remaining between Emma and me.

"Don't feel badly," reassured Uncle Ed, "I have a lot more experience than you at this game."

I didn't care who won. It had been fun.

"I think we can try the beach now," said Uncle Ed. "Grab your jackets."

We opened the door and were greeted with — "Spindrift! It's spindrift," I yelled.

The rough sea was churning up huge waves and sending spindrift to meet us. "That feels good," I said, "and I can even taste the salt."

Emma and I ran ahead, eager to be on the beach again. The tide, although not yet full, was already many feet farther up the beach than any previous high tide we had seen. All along its edge was seaweed and unknown treasures, as Uncle Ed told us, washed up for our investigation.

We started poking through the tangled masses of seaweed and debris. "Look at all the shells," I said.

"And look at the driftwood," added Emma. "But what made all those holes in it?"

"The shipworm did that drilling," answered Uncle Ed. "He does a great deal of damage to anything wooden that's in the sea, but you can't deny that his tunnels are an amazing piece of artwork.

He isn't really a worm at all but a boring clam Notice how the tunnels never touch each other, even when they are crowded together."

"I found a sea urchin," I called. I was glad I had taken the time to study that pile of seaweed, since this was the first urchin I had seen on the beach.

"Uncle Ed, look at this driftwood," said Emma, "You said that shipworm holes didn't touch, but look at this."

"Thought you caught me, didn't you, Emma," laughed Uncle Ed. "A shipworm didn't do that drilling. These holes do join each other. Notice also that they are larger, and not as uniform in size as the shipworm holes.

A different kind of borer did this work. Probably a shelled creature in the isopod family. Hold your hand under it and give that piece a shake."

"Tiny, tiny shells fell out," said Emma. "And look at the other shells in here. See that scallop shell, it's only about a quarter of an inch long."

"Many sea creatures use this kind of driftwood for a home," said Uncle Ed.

"I know Mom would love to have this," said Emma excitedly. "She can hang it on the wall for a decoration."

"How did a coconut get here?" I asked in amazement.

"The ocean currents carried that coconut to our beach, Ryan," answered Uncle Ed. "The currents are like rivers in the sea. Unlike the tides and the waves that move water onto our shores, the currents move up and down the coast, paralleling the shore."

"What causes the currents?" asked Emma.

"The ocean currents are caused chiefly by the winds, continued Uncle Ed. "Other factors also influence the currents. When the sun heats the ocean surface near the equator the water becomes lighter and tends to flow toward the poles. The cold, heavy water from the poles then flows toward the equator in subsurface currents.

The earth's rotation greatly influences all moving things, causing the currents to go toward the right in the northern hemisphere and to the left in the southern hemisphere. The location of land masses causes the currents to change their direction also."

"It sounds confusing," I said.

"Well, it is a little complicated, I'll admit," said Uncle Ed. "But you should try to understand it since it is such an important influence on both the oceans and the land.

Much of our weather results from interactions of currents. The Japan Current warms the northwestern part of the United States, while the Gulf Stream warms the northeastern part of our country. Where these warm currents flow the ocean water can be warmer than expected.

I had an interesting experience while visiting Prince Edward Island some years ago. We had visited Maine first and found the water much too cold for any lengthy swimming. But when we got to PEI the water was surprisingly warm, about 72. This is because the Gulf Stream warms the shores of PEI even though it is many miles north of Maine, and the Labrador Current cools the shores of Maine.

So geographic location alone isn't the only thing that determines a climate. We can talk about it more, and I think you'll understand it more, by looking at the globe. Remind me of that later."

"Look at the length of this seaweed I found," called Emma. "It's twice as tall as I am."

"That's a piece of kelp, Emma," said Uncle Ed. "They grow much taller than that. They look like a forest of trees in the oceans."

"But for such a big thing it doesn't have any roots," I said with surprise.

"The seaweed doesn't have roots because it doesn't need roots," answered Uncle Ed. "They have something called a 'holdfast' which anchors them in place. Trees and plants on the land have to absorb water and nutrition from the soil and need roots for this, but the seaweed just takes the nutrition directly from the sea water.

Unlike our land plants seaweeds have no flowers either, and therefore no seeds. And they have blades instead of leaves. Like our land trees the seaweeds provide a home and food for many creatures."

We didn't have to walk far to discover more and more fascinating treasures. I probably could have just taken a single tangle of seaweed and spent an hour sorting through all the secrets it held. But the lure of so many piles was too tempting.

I gave each a quick, searching look, took the obvious and best and moved on. Emma was more patient and knelt down and poked and probed. "What have I found?" she asked, holding up a black pouch with a long extension coming from each end.

"That's a skate egg case," said Uncle Ed. Noticing our confused looks he continued. "A skate is a fish. Those little egg cases are sometimes called 'mermaids' purses'. The skate is one of the rays. You have probably seen pictures of manta rays. The skate is a strange looking fellow with a flattish body, a long tail and a large fin on either side of its body.

We were accumulating quite an armload of treasures but couldn't stop the hunt. A white flat object caught my eye. I hoped it would be a sand dollar, and it Was; unbroken and bleached by the sun and salt. I carefully placed it in my pocket hoping this fragile skeleton wouldn't break.

Emma came running over, "I've found a sand dollar." We compared our finds and they were almost identical. I was glad she had found one too.

The sky was clearing, the sun was setting and we reluctantly headed back to Spindrift. We looked so funny parading across the sand, arms overloaded and pockets bulging.

I had completely forgotten about the long overdue dinner. We had a simple meal of tuna fish salad which we really enjoyed.

"The currents are really streams of life," said Uncle Ed, "because they transport sea life from one area to another. Let's look at the globe. The arrows show the direction of the major ocean currents. You could throw a bottle overboard here off the coast of North Africa and the current could bring it to the Gulf Stream and onto our beach."

I examined the globe and followed the arrows. "If someone or something floated from the coast of South America in the Humboldt Current, could they land over here in the Pacific Ocean?"

"That very thing was proved by the famous voyage of the Kon-Tiki to Tahiti," replied Uncle Ed. "And the tuna fish you like so much, it was probably caught here near Peru. Can you tell whether tuna likes warm or cold currents?"

"Cold," we answered immediately, seeing the arrows that showed the current off Peru had come up from the cold South Pole.

I hadn't actually studied a globe before and it was really interesting. I got a much better understanding of the placement of different countries in relation to others. I decided to ask Dad if I could move the globe he had in his office to my bedroom. I'd like to learn more about the earth's geography.

"I'm sorry to have to remind you," said Uncle Ed reluctantly, "but bedtime was an hour ago. Did you have a good day, Ryan, in spite of the rain?"

"It was a great day, Uncle Ed," I answered with a grateful grin. "Thanks."

Day Five

I woke up to the sound of voices — Emma and Uncle Ed laughing together in the kitchen. Afraid I was missing something I ran to join them.

"Glad you're up, Ryan," said Uncle Ed.

"I'm glad too," said Emma. "Now we can eat. I'm starving!"

"I'm sure you are both starving, as usual. And today we can eat leisurely. I promised you some fishing and today's the day. But since we're fishermen for a day we have to follow the rhythm of the tide."

"Fishing! In a boat? When do we leave?" I asked excitedly.

Low tide will be about noon today and we stand a better chance of finding ourselves some fish by waiting for the incoming tide. The fish are more active then because the tide brings with it a new supply of food. Hopefully, we can boat a few good eating fish, but there's no guarantee."

"What's the name of your boat," asked Emma.

"I call her the 'Becky-Bee'," answered Uncle Ed.

"Becky-Bee!" said Emma. "Now I remember. Sometimes instead of Beverly, you called her Bee. You named your boat for both of your daughters. I wish someone would name a boat after me."

With a laugh Uncle Ed replied, "I'll name my next boat after you. O.K.?"
Emma laughed too. "Uncle Ed found an album of really old pictures that we can look at after breakfast, Ryan."

"Emma, you make the pictures and your uncle sound ancient. The snapshots were taken when the twins were about your age — not so long ago.

I got my first camera when I was about your age, Ryan. One of the first pictures I took was of your Dad, when he was a baby. I loved using my camera. Taking pictures was very different back then. I worked mowing lawns with a push lawn mower and doing other errands to earn the money for the film and developing costs.

You never knew how your pictures turned out until you took the roll of film to a photo shop that developed the film. They had equipment that turned the roll of film into the photos in these albums.

I spent hours putting albums of pictures together. I still have many of them, too. Since the beach isn't the best place to store photographs, I left many of them in my old bedroom with your Grandma and Grandpa.

I'm sure I love nature and the beach so much because my parents were such enthusiastic campers and travelers. Even when your Dad was very young the family explored many of the National Parks. He was a good camper, too. Your Aunts and their families still camp regularly.

We will all be together in September and I'll share the old albums. That will be fun."

As we ate, we talked about the memories of trips and summer vacations that Uncle Ed had captured on film. "There is a series of photos taken in Canada that you should find especially interesting," said Uncle Ed. "We had gone camping in Nova Scotia. I wanted to see the great tides in the Minas Basin so we picked a campsite nearby. Sheer luck had us there during a spring tide. It's an experience I'll never forget."

"What's so special about the tides in the Minas Basin?" I asked.

"Well, Ryan, they're the highest tides on earth," answered Uncle Ed. "I saw them rise over fifty feet in a matter of a few hours and it was quite a sight. When we finished breakfast, we'll go out on the porch and look at the album."

Sitting comfortable with Uncle Ed between us we began to page through the book of photographs. There were pictures of Aunt Barbara and Uncle Ed when they were first married; pictures of beaches, lighthouses, mountains, pictures of cousins Becky and Bev when they were babies.

"Wait until you see the next section," said Uncle Ed.

"There's your father when he was your age."

"I don't believe it," said Emma. "He looks so young."

"Yes, Emma," laughed Uncle Ed. "He really was young once. Why I can even remember when he was born. Children find it hard to believe that their parents were ever young. But now you've seen the proof."

"Where was that picture taken?" I asked.

"That was on a trip to Prince Edward Island, in Canada. Lovely Place."

"Look at the funny clothes," laughed Emma.

"And the hair," I added.

"They do look a little funny compared to today's styles, agreed Uncle Ed, "but at the time they were very nice. Now we are coming to the pictures of those extreme tides."

I turned the page and stared. "I don't believe it," I said.

Spread out before us were 24 pictures, with notes saying they were taken at 30- minute intervals over a 12-hour period. In shot #1 a ship was docked at a pier looking very normal.

Each following picture showed the water lowering until the ship seemed to be sitting in mud. If it hadn't been securely tied to the dock it would surely have tipped over.

"I've never seen a picture like that before," said Emma. "Even the ship's propeller is out of water. What are those slat-like things under the boat?"

"That is to prevent the ship from settling into the mud at low tide, Emma. The captain of this ship let us on board and one of the crewmen took our picture. I wanted to have all of us in this one.

We then stayed to watch the tide return the ship to a normal-looking floating position. The people in the area are used to this display of tidal power but it is really a tremendous sight to witness. It was like filling and then draining a bathtub."

"What causes such extreme tides?" I asked.

"Nova Scotia is a peninsula to the north of Maine that juts into the Atlantic Ocean like a huge pier. The Bay of Fundy that curves around Nova Scotia forms a funnel like area. And as the walls of the bay narrow, the height and the flow of the water increases greatly. But don't take my word for it. Check out the shape of the Bay and the Province of Nova Scotia on the globe later and I think you'll get the idea.

I felt very humble watching this great tidal force that man had never been able to harness. Many imaginative scientists in the past have dreamed of controlling this force to produce electrical energy and progress has been made.

It is very complicated. Each tidal area is unique and problems with protecting sea life from harm have to be solved. One concern is the noise in the water that affects many sea creatures. Hopefully scientists will solve the problems and you will see the dream of tidal power before you are old and gray like me."

"Uncle Ed gave us an affectionate hug and we continued browsing through the album. There were many pictures taken at Spindrift during summer vacations with Uncle Ed's family.

Emma looked thoughtful and asked, "This is a real neat place in the summer, Uncle Ed, but isn't it lonesome in the winter?"

"Well, it's different in the winter," said Uncle Ed. "Your Aunt Barb and I had planned to live here after I retired. We used to spend many weekends here and loved it in all weather, but after her death I had second thoughts about living here alone, especially in the winter. I tried it out for a few months before I sold my house in the city."

"Do you have any neighbors here in the winter?" I asked.

"Well, many of the Lucky Lane Gang are here all year and we have a strong bond of friendship and support. We have fewer neighbors in the winter. Some are retired people like myself while others are people born and raised in the area. We have a common love for the shore.

We are always ready to help when needed. I'm not the best plumber but Fred, who lives in the gray house by the Post Office, is a great plumber. We all pool out talents and share in many ways.

When Doris does her baking, Dave always arrives with some goodies for me. You don't have to live physically close to people to be good neighbors.

"What do you do all winter long?" I asked.

Long before winter, as soon as the school year begins, I work as a substitute teacher in that busy community you past across the channel. I love being back in the classroom.

And now that I have the time, I'm finally writing that biology textbook I've always wanted to write. When I need a break to clear my mind, I take a walk on the beach, no matter what the weather. It has a very interesting effect, both soothing and invigorating and I come back eager to get on with my work."

"Does anybody come to visit you?" Emma asked.

"My daughters come quite often and usually bring a friend or two. We have great times together. I'd be happy to have the two of you visit during the winter when you have a few days of vacation. The beach is different then and few people get to enjoy it. Just be sure to bring your warm clothes.

And one very special treat can only be enjoyed by the winter residents, and even then, it is usually a very brief treat — that's snow on the beach. Watching the surf eat into the snow and walking through this unusual mixture is a very exciting experience.

Look at the time! We've talked so long, now we will have to grab our fishing gear and head for the Bay."

"We're going fishing! I called for all to hear. "We're going fishing!"

Spindrift is about a ten- minute drive from the bay. It has a real name but everyone always called it 'the Bay". On the way over we talked about our destination. "You've seen and read about bays, I'm sure," said Uncle Ed, "but what is a bay and how is it different from the shore or the open ocean?"

"A bay," I said, "is a place where the ocean comes into the land and is surrounded by land. It's a place where fishing boats and crab and oyster boats and just fun kinds of boats dock at night. It's busy, as busy as a town, but with boats instead of cars."

"The bay is different to me," said Emma, "It's a place of calmness. It is a quiet place where boats stay because the water is protected. I think it's a peaceful place even though there are a lot of busy people around."

"I like both of your answers," said Uncle Ed, "and put together we have the whole idea of a bay and what it offers people. What about the animal life at the bay?"

"I'll bet there are different things there," I said. "Animals that prefer calm water instead of waves."

"I'm sure the birds like it," added Emma.

"You're both right again," said Uncle Ed. "And birds, like boats, seek safety here in harsh weather." And with a laugh he added, "The gulls are always there to feed on the fish heads and waste the fishermen throw overboard. It would be a messy place without the scavenger gulls."

The bay was just ahead; and we could already see the gulls, sitting around, walking around, flying around, gliding around in the air in great circles waiting for their handouts. Uncle Ed parked his car at the dock, "Bet you don't have a parking lot like this one at home," he asked.

We didn't. This parking area was made mostly of shells -- millions of clam, oyster and scallop shells that had been dumped, spread, crushed and packed down.

"That's a good idea," I remarked. "You don't have to repair it either. Just dump some more shells and the cars take care of the rest."

"Well, we have a better use for the oyster shells now," said Uncle Ed." They are recycled to make homes for new oysters."

A shop at dockside said Barnacle Bill's Baits, and we walked in. There were baits of all kinds; live minnows in tanks, sand worms and clams in cardboard containers, frozen squid in blocks like bricks and dozens of artificial lures of all sizes, shapes and colors. We selected worms, squid and clams and headed for the dock.

"Notice the pilings that support the dock," said Uncle Ed. "What do you see?"

We could see at once that there were stripes, "Like the rocks at the tide pool." said Emma.

"You can really see the difference between high and low tide on these pilings," I said. "It's almost like a thermometer."

Uncle Ed laughed, "That's a good comparison, Ryan. And while you're looking that way, do you see anything else interesting in the mud over there?"

We could see dozens of small, dark crabs, some with one very large claw and one small claw, others with two small claws. "Here are the fiddler crabs," said Uncle Ed. "They live in burrows in the mud and are only active at low tide. Care to guess how they got their name?"

"That's easy," answered Emma. "That big claw looks sort of like a fiddle."

"And I'll guess that the males are the ones with the big claws," I offered.

"I just noticed something," Said Emma excitedly, "Some of them have big claws on the right and some on the left. Why?"

"That's a good observation, Emma," said Uncle Ed. "Most will have a large left claw but if he should lose it in a fight, he will grow a large one on the right. Many sea creatures can regenerate lost parts. Remember that four-legged sea-star at the tidal pool? He will soon regrow a fifth leg.

"And here we have the Becky-Bee. How's that for a boat?"

"Well," I said, "it's a lot smaller than most of the other boats. And there's water in the bottom."

"It's small but seaworthy, Ryan," said Uncle Ed. "Remember we had a heavy rain yesterday. Bailing the boat is usually the first job when you go fishing. In you go now. Here's a bailer for each of you."

"That's a funny bailer — it's a horseshoe crab shell," said Emma in surprise.

"It's a very handy and efficient bailer," said Uncle Ed. "And if one gets lost, I can always find another. Now let me help you with those lifejackets. This boat doesn't leave the dock until we all have on our life jackets. They are to a boat what seat belts are to a car and the sea is our highway today."

We bailed while Uncle Ed eased the boat out of the dock area. "We have time to go for a ride around the bay before we fish," said Uncle Ed. "The tide is still very low."

"I was hoping we could do that," I said with a happy smile as the boat headed across the calm, sparkling water. We watched with delight as the wake behind the boat got higher as our speed increased.

"What kind of sailors are you?" questioned Uncle Ed. "Do you know what the front of the boat is called."

"The bow," I shouted.

"And the back?" said Uncle Ed.

"The stem," Emma and I chorused. And before Uncle Ed had a chance to ask another question, I called out, "Starboard is the right side and port is the left."

"Very good! It's nice to know I have seamen aboard," laughed Uncle Ed.

"Not really," I said reluctantly. "A friend of ours has a boat and he told us those things, but I don't understand how you know where you're going in the water. I mean there are no lines down the center of a road or any street signs. Isn't it confusing?"

"It can be confusing, Ryan, until you become familiar with the 'rules of the road' for the waterways," answered Uncle Ed. "The rules are similar to the highway rules and should be studied by everyone who operates a boat.

We'll see some buoys later and I'll point them out to you. They help to direct traffic. No buoys are needed in this part of our bay."

It was a perfect day for a boat ride; the blue sky was dotted with cottony cumulus clouds; the bay waters reflected many shades of green. The spray felt cool and refreshing against my skin. I put my hand in the water and let it bounce along, enjoying the coolness.

Uncle Ed cut back on the engine as we neared the opposite shore. We slowly eased passed beach houses dotting the shoreline. We could see people on many of the docks. We waved and they waved back. Some children were pulling in a crab net. From their excitement we knew they had caught a crab.

We glided by sailboats gently bobbing at anchor. A boat pulling a water skier speeded passed and we bounced in their wake. Looking down we could see seaweeds reaching upward. Even fish could be seen darting among the seaweed.

Ahead was a marina lined with many boats and much activity. We carefully threaded our way through the traffic. We were now passing the lower end of the bay and heading along the side from which we had started. Fewer houses were along this shoreline that was bordered with thick cattails and reeds. We could see the road we had driven to the dock; just ahead and growing bigger was the sign for Barnacle Bill's Baits.

There was more activity on the dock now and we could read from the water line on the pilings that the tide was rising. Many small boats were preparing to leave the dock; the quiet, calm bay was becoming a busy, active bay.

We passed the pier and headed toward the mouth of the bay, becoming part of a miniature boat caravan. Everyone had a favorite fishing spot and we were soon at Uncle Ed's.

"Think you can lower the anchor yourself, Ryan?" asked Uncle Ed.

I felt proud that he trusted me with that important job and gently lowered the anchor until we were "dead in the water" and ready to fish.

"Let's hope there are some hungry flounder down on the bottom," said Uncle Ed as he opened the bait. "The flounders are bottom feeders and will probably like the worms or clams, but the choice is yours."

I selected some clam but Emma chose a worm, "1 should have warned you," said Uncle Ed looking at Emma, "that all fishermen and fisherwomen have to bait their own hooks.'

Emma hesitated, made a funny face and then said, "I'll do it if you'll show me how."

"I'll show both of you how to bait your hooks with the different baits and then you're on your own."

Uncle Ed threaded a piece of worm on one of Emma's two hooks and then handed her a piece of wiggly worm. This was a strange spiny worm, not like our garden variety, and I was glad I had chosen a clam.

It was fun to watch Emma intently concentrating on putting that wiggly thing on the hook. Her patience paid off and she triumphantly lowered her line.

We sat quietly for a few minutes until I suddenly called out "I've got something."

"Me, too," said Emma excitedly.

"So do I," said Uncle Ed. "Reel them in."

The fish didn't fight much, my line just felt heavy. "What is it?" I asked in amazement. At the end of my line was a funny flat fish with both eyes on his top, dark side. He was very light-colored underneath.

"You've got a nice flounder, Ryan. He's a good eating fish," said Uncle Ed, "but look what I've got."

A large crab hung from Uncle Ed's bait. As he neared the top, he released his grip and paddled away.

"I've got a flounder, too," cried Emma. "This is fun!"

"Do you have a stringer to put the fish on?" I asked, as he removed the hook from the fish.

"I have a different method," answered Uncle Ed. "All fishermen have their own pet way of catching and handling fish and I have mine." He reached into his tackle box and took out a small, but heavy looking stick.

"This might seem cruel at first but I figure if I'm going to kill the fish anyway, I'd prefer not to let him suffer." With that he gave the fish a sharp rap on the head between the eyes and we could see that the fish was dead. "Some people say that fish can't feel pain. I can't agree and I prefer this way. You have to use the method you are comfortable with. Uncle Ed put the dead fish in a canvas bag, thoroughly wet the bag and put the bag under his seat.

The strange looking fish you caught started his life looking like most other fish. He had an eye on either side and swam in the same manner as do most fish. But then he got much wider than he was deep and became a flatfish. When he was quite young one eye moved to its present position. Another unusual thing he can do is to change the markings on his back to match his surroundings enabling him to hide from his enemies on the bottom of the bay."

"Got another one," called Emma as she reeled in a small flounder.

"He's a little too small to keep, Emma," said Uncle Ed. "Let's give him a chance to grow up." He wet his hands thoroughly before handling the fish and unhooked him carefully. We watched him swim away from the boat with mixed emotions.

"Why did you get your hands wet first?" asked Emma.

"If you're going to return a fish to the water it is very important that you handle him carefully. Fish have a slimy, mucous covering. This, along with scales, protects them from attack by disease, parasites and such. Wet hands help to prevent removal of the protective covering on the fish. An injured fish must use his food to repair his body before he can grow larger."

"I've got a problem, Uncle Ed," I said.

"I can see that you have a problem," said Uncle Ed, looking at my tangled line. "Take my rod while I work on yours."

I watched gratefully as Uncle Ed unraveled the jumble of line. Suddenly I felt a nibble and knew I had a heavy fish on Uncle Ed's line. "Reel her in," called Uncle Ed.

Excitedly I cranked the reel handle until a huge, at least to me, flounder came in view. "Let me get the net for that beauty," said Uncle Ed. "That's a good one."

I felt both proud and guilty but Uncle Ed didn't seem to mind at all as he put my catch in the bag, wet it again and passed me my untangled line.

Flounder fishing got a little slow and Uncle Ed suggested we try jigging for some bluefish. A jig is an artificial lure that is moved just under the surface of the water by jerks on the rod. This kind of action attracts many kinds of surface feeding fish.

Jigging was harder than it looked but we finally got the idea just as Uncle Ed yelled, "got one." A fighting fish was pulling furiously at the line. "Get the net ready," called Uncle Ed. "Head first with him, Ryan." I was so excited I was afraid I'd do something wrong, but in he went and we had our first bluefish.

"I thought from the way he was fighting that he would be huge," said Emma.

"A 'blue' is a strong fish," said Uncle Ed. "Great fun to --"

"I've got one, I've got one," I yelled. The rod shook and quivered and I had to hold it with all my might to keep from losing it. It was a tremendous feeling of strength all the way from the fish, up the line and through me. The fish darted left and right, up and down but was finally close enough for Uncle Ed to net him.

"Great work, Ryan," said Uncle Ed with a smile. "Now it's your turn, Emma."

I felt too thrilled even to speak. I had trouble getting my jigging coordinated again but it didn't matter now; I had caught a bluefish.

Emma's patience paid off in a yell of surprise — "Uncle Ed! Look!"

Another bluefish was fighting capture. Uncle Ed carefully moved next to Emma. "If you need help, I'm right here," he said.

The fish continued to dart across the water with Emma determined to land him herself. She finally said, "I guess I need help."

"I'll just hold the rod, you do the reeling," said Uncle Ed. The combination worked and we had another blue. Emma looked exhausted, excited and happy.

"That's what I call a good catch," laughed Uncle Ed. "Let's call it a day and let someone else have a turn. I promised to show you the buoys. The current in the channel is too strong for our little boat so we won't attempt to navigate it but you'll be able to see from a distance."

The engine churned. We moved through the water until we could see buoys, some red and some black. Uncle Ed slowed the engine. "We don't want to be here long," he said. "It's going to get busy very soon, since the fishing boats are coming back. Notice the buoys. They show the side to pass when you are going in a given direction.

The three R's of navigation are Red Right Returning. When a boat is coming from seaward the red buoys should be on its right side, black on the left. Of course, it reverses when you are going out to sea.

"Are the buoys always the same shape?" I asked.

"No," answered Uncle Ed. "Buoys come in many shapes, and combinations of colors, most are numbered, some have flashing lights, some gongs, whistles, or horns. The important thing for anyone using these waterways is to use and understand navigation maps. They list the buoys and other markers. It's not much fun to be lost on the water. There's no local convenience store to ask advice."

We left the channel and rode past many boats quite similar to Uncle Ed's. They were still fishing and we didn't get too close. Some people waved, others held up stringers heavy with fish.

Large fishing boats were returning to their docks in the bay crowded with people. I hoped that they had had a good fishing day too. Our dock was ahead and we were soon safely docked with gear unloaded.

Everyone on the dock was eager to share fish stories about the ones that did and the ones that didn't get away. We were no exception and •enthusiastically added our own fish story.

We climbed into the car, filling it with the smell of fish. "First thing on the list when we get home is to clean the fish," said Uncle Ed. "It will be a rather messy chore but a necessary one for every fisherman. Fish spoil quickly so it's a job we can't stall."

The ride back to Spindrift seemed so much shorter than the ride to the dock. We gathered Uncle Ed's fish cleaning supplies and walked down to the beach.

"Why do the fish still feel cold, Uncle Ed?" asked Emma. "The air is so hot outside."

"I've been keeping these fish cold by a method called refrigeration by evaporation," said Uncle Ed. "You noticed that I kept the bag wet. When water evaporates it uses up heat and cools whatever is wet."

"I don't understand what you mean." replied Emma. "Can you give us an example?"

"I'll try," said Uncle Ed. "I'm sure you've enjoyed the cooling effect of a fan. Well besides just blowing air around, the fan causes perspiration on our skin to evaporate more quickly. The heat needed for this evaporation is taken from our body and we are cooled.

If there was no electricity for refrigerators, it would be possible, although impractical, to cool our food by keeping it constantly wet and always evaporating water."

"That's interesting," said Emma, "and simple to do when you're fishing."

We placed the fish, a board, a scaler and a sharp knife down at the water's edge. "Scaling the fish comes first," said Uncle Ed. "I'll show you how to do it and then you can take a turn."

I tried to imitate Uncle Ed's easy motions but I had trouble. "Don't get discouraged, Ryan," said Uncle Ed. "I made it look easy because I've done it so many times." Scales were flying everywhere; they stuck to us like glue.

When I got tired Emma tried her hand at scaling. We still had most of the fish to do and were completely exhausted and Uncle Ed had to finish the job.

The sharp-eyed gulls had noticed us and were gathering for a feast. Uncle Ed showed us how to remove the guts from the fish, then the fins and lastly the head. We put some of the fish waste in a pile a little distance from where we were working to draw the gulls. They were getting so anxious that they were crowding around us and making the work more difficult.

We were finally done and ready to cook some of the fish and freeze the rest. The gulls lost no time in cleaning the beach. "It's handy having the gulls around," I said. "No garbage cans to empty, no fish waste to smell and pollute the air."

We all helped with dinner which was a feast fit for a king — or queen. Fish never tasted better.

The sun set red in the sky and we knew tomorrow would be another good day — our last at Spindrift "You can't go home without having seen a sunrise from the beach," said Uncle Ed. "Want me to wake you early tomorrow?"

"That would be great," I said, and Emma added, "We've never seen a sunrise."

"Tomorrow you will," said Uncle Ed, giving us an affectionate pat. "Better be early to bed tonight, though. Pleasant dreams."

Day Six

"Ryan, Emma. Sunrise in twenty minutes."

The voice, though soft, seemed to fill the semidarkness in our bedroom. Half asleep, I could just make out the face of Uncle Ed.

"I promised to wake you in time to see the sunrise but you seem too sleepy. Better roll over and get some more rest."

"No, no," I protested, scrambling out of bed, "I'm not sleepy any more. We'll be ready in a minute," Emma, too, was now out of bed and groping around for her clothes. "Don't go down to the beach without us," she called.

"No fear of that," reassured Uncle Ed. "Glad you decided to get up. Your first sunrise is guaranteed to make this a special day."

Outdoors now the day already felt special. "We could have watched the show from the porch," said Uncle Ed, "but it somehow means more to me to be here on the beach. I've enjoyed the sunrise in many different places and settings but I think I like it best across an expanse of ocean."

We settled ourselves on the beach blanket that Uncle Ed had brought along, since the sand was very damp. We were alone except for the parading gulls and a distant figure far down the beach with a dog close by.

The sky had a look unlike any we had ever seen before. We sat and waited. Everything was suddenly quiet — as if all of nature hushed to await the arrival of Her Majesty, the Sun. We felt our excitement mount. The sky glowed with a soft pink light; everything was bathed in this radiance. Our eyes were glued to the flat, distant horizon. We knew the moment was near.

A red sliver was suddenly on the horizon. How marvelous to watch the sun inch its way into the cloudless sky. The sun, the center of our universe, had returned for another day.

With the sunrise had come activity. The birds took to the sky and soared; the thunder of the high tide applauded this great moment.

Emma and I sat quietly fingering the sand as the sun continued its climb. Its color would turn more and more yellow; we would no longer be able to safely look at it. I wanted to speak but could not.

Sensing my feelings, Uncle Ed said, "That was quite a show, wasn't it, Ryan? No matter how often I've seen it, it never fails to kind of overwhelm me with emotion. Do you feel that way, too?"

I nodded. This was a very special day already, with a moment I'd never forget. Looking around at the other cottages, their shades still drawn, I felt sadness for the people still sleeping. They had missed that moment. They would soon be up and about enjoying the sun's warmth, but they had missed the sunrise. Even if it meant a nap later in the day, the sunrise was worth it.

We ate breakfast slowly, wanting to stretch the time left at Spindrift.

"I have to go to the store in a few minutes. Why don't you two take a last walk on the beach and enjoy this time alone — soak up all of the sights and sounds you can to last until your next visit," suggested Uncle Ed. "I won't be gone for too long."

To surprise Uncle Ed, we decided to return the cottage to the neat way it looked when we arrived. We would take our walk as soon as our work was done. So much of the untidiness was from our things scattered around. Uncle Ed had said the house had really looked "lived in" this week and he liked that, but we would enjoy our walk more if we earned it.

Brooms, dustpans and enthusiasm soon had Spindrift clean and tidy. We packed our bags, taking special care with treasures we had gathered for Mom and Dad. Looking around we saw that our job was done and we felt good.

"Let's go," I called to Emma. "Race you to the beach." Happily, we ran across the sands. I decided to sit and rest for a few minutes while Emma walked alone along the sand.

Although it seemed the edge of two worlds, the land and the water, I knew now that there really was no edge here, but a blending and a living that each exchanged with the other.

I watched Emma as she picked something up, examined it and put it in her pocket. A few minutes later she knelt down, looking closely at the sand. What had attracted her I wondered? Next, she skimmed a few shells into the surf, watching them bounce and then drop to the bottom.

She was enjoying simple pleasures of the beach. We had shared so many things this past week and we had grown closer together. I hoped this closeness would continue.

Emma was now walking toward me; I could tell that she had an idea. "I've been thinking, Ryan. Let's make a thank you note for Uncle Ed. It will be hard to say all the things we'll want to say, but we can try."

"Good idea," I agreed, "And let's make it a poem like his invitation to us. I'll run up to Spindrift and get a pad and paper. Be back in a minute."

And so, at the edge of the sea we wrote:

It was nice to be with you here.
    We hope we have brought you cheer.

You've taught us about the ocean and sand
    And how the wind and sea affect each land.

We won't forget the times we've walked
    And looked and watched and how you talked
Always to us and asking us too
    To share our ideas with you.

To share, we've learned, is the greatest way
    To live and learn throughout the day.

Like the land shares itself with the sea
> With people and pets, it should also be.

So, thank you, thank you
> For a wonderful time.

You've shared yourself
> It's all we could ask for.

Emma and Ryan

"Now that it's finished, where should we put it," asked Emma, "where Uncle Ed will find.

"Someplace he's sure to look. How about on his desk or in the cupboard?" I suggested.

"How about in the refrigerator?" laughed Emma.

"In the refrigerator," I agreed, "'next to the milk. And so, it was decided and we returned to Spindrift and awaited the proper time to hide our note.

Uncle Ed returned and marveled at the transformation that Spindrift had undergone. We busied ourselves preparing lunch; the menu was fish chowder, and muffins. We were very proud of how much we had learned to do around the kitchen. Would Mom and Dad really believe we made this meal? — with a little help, of course.

We were so absorbed in our work that we failed to hear the car approach. "Hello there, anyone home?"

"Mom and Dad," we shrieked and ran to meet them, almost knocking them over with our enthusiasm.

"It's good to see you two again," said Dad, giving us a warm hug. "I hope you haven't been giving your uncle here any trouble."

"It would be hard to remember when I've had nicer house guests," smiled Uncle Ed and Emma and I visibly glowed.

"You're both so suntanned," said Mother, "and I think you have grown an inch a piece. We missed you; the house was really quiet, too quiet."

"Something smells good like jellyfish chowder," said Dad. We all laughed. That was Uncle Ed's nickname for his favorite fish chowder.

"I thought you'd forgotten that little joke," laughed Uncle Ed.

"No, never!" said Dad. "And another thing, I probably didn't appreciate all the fun and knowledge my big brother gave me at the time, but Ed, you sure taught me a thing or two. That's why I was so glad to have Emma and Ryan receive your invitation."

Looking at us, "I was one of your Uncle's 'experiments' in teaching. He tried all his theories out on me. So, if he became a good teacher, I should get at least some of the credit."

"Thanks Bob. You were always a good student, but," with a wink, "your children are better."

Lunch was a happy, noisy time of sharing the experiences and memories of the past few days, enjoying them anew in the retelling.

Down on the beach for the last time, we bubbled with information, facts and feelings, in an almost endless flow of words.

And then too soon it was time for farewells. Emma hung behind to slip our note in the refrigerator while I busied Uncle Ed with a few questions. We were all in the car and about to "buckle up" when, "Hold on," said Uncle Ed. "Nearly forgot something."

With dismay we watched him head straight for the refrigerator — and open the freezer section. "Here is some of the catch from our fishing expedition. They'll make a nice meal. Just ask the children to fix them for you. They know how."

And then good-byes, but not for long. We promised to visit again soon. Uncle Ed waved us out of sight. We were headed for home.

Had it only been six days at the seashore. We had enjoyed and learned so much. The gentle rocking of the car was making me drowsy. My eyelids felt very heavy. Next to me, Emma was already asleep, with a smile on her face.

Happy thoughts started flooding my mind — the creatures of the tidal pool, the dunes, fishing from the boat, sandpipers chasing waves, popcorn in front of the fireplace during the storm, today's sunrise. And a part of each happy thought was Uncle Ed.

Happy thoughts blended and melted together. They would be a part of many pleasant thoughts, waking or sleeping for a long time to come. They were all memories of a special time — memories of a seashore, Spindrift memories.